David and Bethsabe by George Peele

Performed c. 1596. First Published 1599

The love of King David and Fair Bethsabe.

With the Tragedie of Absalon.

As it hath ben diuers times plaied on the stage.

http://elizabethandrama.org/wp-content/uploads/2018/10/David-and-Bethsabe-Play-Alone.htm

Index of Contents

DRAMATIS PERSONAE

David and his Family:

David, King of Israel and Judah.
Cusay, a lord, and follower of David.
Amnon, son of David by Ahinoam
Jethray, Servant to Amnon.

Chileab, son of David by Abigail.
Absalon, son of David by Maacah.
Thamar, daughter of David by Maacah.
Adonia, son of David by Haggith.
Salomon, son of David by Bethsabe.
Joab, captain of the host to David, and nephew of
David and son of his sister Zeruia.
Abisai, nephew of David and son of his sister Zeruia.
Amasa, nephew of David and son of his sister Abigail; also captain of the host to Absalon.
Jonadab, nephew of David and son of his brother
Shimeah; also friend to Amnon.

Other Characters:
Urias, a warrior in David's army.
Bethsabe, wife of Uriah.
Maid to Bethsabe.
Nathan, a prophet.
Sadoc, high-priest.
Ahimaas, his son.
Abiathar, a priest.
Jonathan, his son.
Achitophel, chief counsellor to Absalon.
Ithay, a Captain from Gath.
Semei.
Hanon, King of Ammon.
Machaas, King of Gath.
Woman of Thecoa.
Messenger, Soldiers, Shepherds, and Attendants.
Concubines to David.
Chorus.

PROLOGUS

Of Israel's sweetest singer now I sing,
His holy style and happy victories;
Whose Muse was dipt in that inspiring dew
Arch-angels stillèd from the breath of Jove,
Decking her temples with the glorious flowers
Heavens rained on tops of Sion and Mount Sinai.
Upon the bosom of his ivory lute
The cherubins and angels laid their breasts;
And, when his consecrated fingers strook
The golden wires of his ravishing harp,
He gave alarum to the host of Heaven,
That, winged with lightning, brake the clouds, and cast
Their crystal armour at his conquering feet.
Of this sweet poet, Jove's musiciän,

And of his beauteous son, I prease to sing.
Then help, divine Adonai, to conduct
Upon the wings of my well-tempered verse
The hearers' minds above the towers of Heaven,
And guide them so in this thrice-haughty flight,
Their mounting feathers scorch not with the fire
That none can temper but thy holy hand:
To thee for succour flies my feeble Muse,
And at thy feet her iron pen doth use.

[The **PROLOGUE-SPEAKER**, before going out, draws a curtain and discovers **BETHSABE**, with her **MAID**, bathing over a spring: she sings, and **DAVID** sits above viewing her.

SCENE I

The Royal Palace, Jerusalem.

DAVID sitting on the Palace roof, watching **BETHSABE** below bathing over a spring.

THE SONG.
Hot sun, cool fire, tempered with sweet air,
Black shade, fair nurse, shadow my white hair:
Shine, sun; burn, fire; breathe, air, and ease me;
Black shade, fair nurse; shroud me, and please me:
Shadow, my sweet nurse, keep me from burning,
Make not my glad cause cause of mourning.
Let not my beauty's fire
Inflame unstaid desire,
Nor pierce any bright eye
That wandereth lightly.

BETHSABE
Come, gentle Zephyr, tricked with those perfumes
That erst in Eden sweetened Adam's love,
And stroke my bosom with thy silken fan:
This shade, sun-proof, is yet no proof for thee;
Thy body, smoother than this waveless spring,
And purer than the substance of the same,
Can creep through that his lances cannot pierce:
Thou, and thy sister, soft and sacred Air,
Goddess of life, and governess of health,
Keep every fountain fresh and arbour sweet;
No brazen gate her passage can repulse,
Nor bushly thicket bar thy subtle breath:
Then deck thee with thy loose delightsome robes,
And on thy wings bring delicate perfumes,

To play the wantons with us through the leaves.

DAVID
What tunes, what words, what looks, what wonders pierce
My soul, incensèd with a sudden fire?
What tree, what shade, what spring, what paradise,
Enjoys the beauty of so fair a dame?
Fair Eva, placed in perfect happiness,
Lending her praise-notes to the liberal heavens,
Strook with the accents of arch-angels' tunes,
Wrought not more pleasure to her husband's thoughts
Than this fair woman's words and notes to mine.
May that sweet plain that bears her pleasant weight
Be still enamelled with discoloured flowers;
That precious fount bear sand of purest gold;
And, for the pebble, let the silver streams
That pierce earth's bowels to maintain the source,
Play upon rubies, sapphires, chrysolites;
The brims let be embraced with golden curls
Of moss that sleeps with sound the waters make
For joy to feed the fount with their recourse;
Let all the grass that beautifies her bower
Bear manna every morn instead of dew,
Or let the dew be sweeter far than that
That hangs, like chains of pearl, on Hermon hill,
Or balm which trickled from old Aaron's beard. –
Cusay, come up, and serve thy lord the king.

[Enter **CUSAY** above.

CUSAY
What service doth my lord the king command?

DAVID
See, Cusay, see the flower of Israel,
The fairest daughter that obeys the king
In all the land the Lord subdued to me;
Fairer than Isaac's lover at the well,
Brighter than inside-bark of new-hewn cedar,
Sweeter than flames of fine-perfumèd myrrh,
And comelier than the silver clouds that dance
On Zephyr's wings before the King of Heaven.

CUSAY
Is it not Bethsabe the Hethite's wife,
Urias now at Rabbah siege with Joab?

DAVID

Go know, and bring her quickly to the king;
Tell her, her graces hath found grace with him.

CUSAY
I will, my lord.

[Exit.

DAVID
Bright Bethsabe shall wash, in David's bower,
In water mixed with purest almond-flower,
And bathe her beauty in the milk of kids:
Bright Bethsabe gives earth to my desires;
Verdure to earth; and to that verdure flowers;
To flowers sweet odours; and to odours wings
That carry pleasures to the hearts of kings.

[Enter **CUSAY**, below, to **BETHSABE**, she starting as something affright.

CUSAY
Fair Bethsabe, the King of Israel
From forth his princely tower hath seen thee bathe;
And thy sweet graces have found grace with him:
Come, then, and kneel unto him where he stands;
The king is gracious, and hath liberal hands.

BETHSABE
Ah, what is Bethsabe to please the king?
Or what is David, that he should desire,
For fickle beauty's sake, his servant's wife?

CUSAY
David, thou know'st, fair dame, is wise and just,
Elected to the heart of Israel's God;
Then do not thou expostulate with him
For any action that contents his soul.

BETHSABE
My lord the king, elect to God's own heart,
Should not his gracious jealousy incense
Whose thoughts are chaste: I hate incontinence.

CUSAY
Woman, thou wrong'st the king, and doubt'st his honour,
Whose truth maintains the crown of Israel,
Making him stay that bade me bring thee straight.

BETHSABE

The king's poor handmaid will obey my lord.

CUSAY
Then come, and do thy duty to his grace;
And do what seemeth favour in his sight.

[Exit, below, with **BETHSABE**.

DAVID
Now comes my lover tripping like the roe,
And brings my longings tangled in her hair.
To joy her love I'll build a kingly bower,
Seated in hearing of a hundred streams,
That, for their homage to her sovereign joys,
Shall, as the serpents fold into their nests
In oblique turnings, wind the[ir] nimble waves
About the circles of her curious walks;
And with their murmur summon easeful sleep
To lay his golden sceptre on her brows. –
Open the doors, and entertain my love;
Open, I say, and, as you open, sing,
Welcome, fair Bethsabe, King David's darling.

[Enter, above, **CUSAY**, with **BETHSABE**.

Welcome, fair Bethsabe, King David's darling.
Thy bones' fair covering, erst discovered fair,
And all mine eyes with all thy beauties pierced:
As Heaven's bright eye burns most when most he climbs
The crookèd zodiac with his fiery sphere,
And shineth furthest from this earthly globe;
So, since thy beauty scorched my conquered soul,
I called thee nearer for my nearer cure.

BETHSABE
Too near, my lord, was your unarmèd heart
When furthest off my hapless beauty pierced;
And would this dreary day had turned to night,
Or that some pitchy cloud had cloaked the sun,
Before their lights had caused my lord to see
His name disparaged and my chastity!

DAVID
My love, if want of love have left thy soul
A sharper sense of honour than thy king,
(For love leads princes sometimes from their seats,)
As erst my heart was hurt, displeasing thee,
So come and taste thy ease with easing me.

BETHSABE
One medicine cannot heal our different harms;
But rather make both rankle at the bone:
Then let the king be cunning in his cure,
Lest flattering both, both perish in his hand.

DAVID
Leave it to me, my dearest Bethsabe,
Whose skill is cónversant in deeper cures. –
And, Cusay, haste thou to my servant Joab,
Commanding him to send Urias home
With all the speed can possibly be used.

CUSAY
Cusay will fly about the king's desire.

[Exeunt.

SCENE II

Before the Walls of the City of Rabbah, the Capital City of Ammon.

Enter **JOAB**, **ABISAI**, **URIAS**, and **OTHERS**, with drum and ensign.

JOAB
Courage, ye mighty men of Israel,
And charge your fatal instruments of war
Upon the bosoms of proud Ammon's son[s],
That have disguised your king's ambassadors,
Cut half their beards and half their garments off,
In spite of Israel and his daughters' sons!
Ye fight the holy battles of Jehovah,
King David's God, and ours, and Jacob's God,
That guides your weapons to their conquering strokes,
Orders your footsteps, and directs your thoughts
To stratagems that harbour victory:
He casts his sacred eyesight from on high,
And sees your foes run seeking for their deaths,
Laughing their labours and their hopes to scorn;
While 'twixt your bodies and their blunted swords
He puts on armour of his honour's proof,
And makes their weapons wound the senseless winds.

ABISAI
Before this city Rabbah we will lie,

And shoot forth shafts as thick and dangerous
As was the hail that Moses mixed with fire,
And threw with fury round about the fields,
Devouring Pharaoh's friends and Egypt's fruits.

URIAS

First, mighty captains, Joab and Abisai,
Let us assault, and scale this kingly tower,
Where all their conduits and their fountains are;
Then we may easily take the city too.

JOAB

Well hath Urias counselled our attempts;
And as he spake us, so assault the tower:
Let Hanon now, the king of Ammon's sons,
Repulse our conquering passage if he dare.

[Enter **HANON**, **MACHAAS**, and **OTHERS**, upon the walls.

HANON

What would the shepherd's-dogs of Israel
Snatch from the mighty issue of King Ammon,
The valiant Ammonites and haughty Syrians?
'Tis not your late successive victories
Can make us yield, or quail our courages;
But if ye dare assay to scale this tower,
Our angry swords shall smite ye to the ground,
And venge our losses on your hateful lives.

JOAB

Hanon, thy father Nahas gave relief
To holy David in his hapless exile,
Livèd his fixèd date, and died in peace:
But thou, instead of reaping his reward,
Hast trod it under foot, and scorned our king;
Therefore thy days shall end with violence,
And to our swords thy vital blood shall cleave.

MACHAAS

Hence, thou that bear'st poor Israel's shepherd's-hook,
The proud lieutenant of that base-born king,
And keep within the compass of his fold;
For, if ye seek to feed on Ammon's fruits,
And stray into the Syrians' fruitful meads,
The mastives of our land shall worry ye,
And pull the weesels from your greedy throats.

ABISAI

Who can endure these pagans' blasphemies?

URIAS
My soul repines at this disparagement.

JOAB
Assault, ye valiant men of David's host,
And beat these railing dastards from their doors.

[Assault, and they win the tower; and then **JOAB** speaks above.

Thus have we won the tower, which we will keep,
Maugre the sons of Ammon and of Syria.

[Enter **CUSAY** below.

CUSAY
Where is Lord Joab, leader of the host?

JOAB
Here is Lord Joab, leader of the host.
Cusay, come up, for we have won the hold.

CUSAY
In happy hour, then, is Cusay come.

[**CUSAY** goes up.

JOAB
What news, then, brings Lord Cusay from the king?

CUSAY
His majesty commands thee out of hand
To send him home Urias from the wars,
For matter of some service he should do.

URIAS
'Tis for no choler hath surprised the king,
I hope, Lord Cusay, 'gainst his servant's truth?

CUSAY
No; rather to prefer Urias' truth.

JOAB
Here, take him with thee, then, and go in peace;
And tell my lord the king that I have fought
Against the city Rabbah with success,
And scalèd where the royal palace is,

The conduit-heads and all their sweetest springs:
Then let him come in person to these walls,
With all the soldiers he can bring besides,
And take the city as his own exploit,
Lest I surprise it, and the people give
The glory of the conquest to my name.

CUSAY
We will, Lord Joab; and great Israel's God
Bless in thy hands the battles of our king!

JOAB
Farewell, Urias; haste away the king.

URIAS
As sure as Joab breathes a victor here,
Urias will haste him and his own return.

[Exeunt **CUSAY** and **URIAS**.

ABISAI
Let us descend, and ope the palace' gate,
Taking our soldiers in to keep the hold.

JOAB
Let us, Abisai: – and, ye sons of Judah,
Be valiant, and maintain your victory.

[Exeunt.

SCENE III

The House of Amnon in Jerusalem.

Enter **AMNON**, **JONADAB**, **JETHRAY**, and Amnon's **PAGE**.

JONADAB
What means my lord, the king's belovèd son,
That wears upon his right triumphant arm
The power of Israel for a royal favour,
That holds upon the tables of his hands
Banquets of honour and all thought's content,
To suffer pale and grisly abstinence
To sit and feed upon his fainting cheeks,
And suck away the blood that cheers his looks?

AMNON

Ah, Jonadab, it is my sister's looks,
On whose sweet beauty I bestow my blood,
That makes me look so amorously lean;
Her beauty having seized upon my heart,
So merely consecrate to her content,
Sets now such guard about his vital blood,
And views the passage with such piercing eyes,
That none can scape to cheer my pining cheeks,
But all is thought too little for her love.

JONADAB

Then from her heart thy looks shall be relieved,
And thou shalt joy her as thy soul desires.

AMNON

How can it be, my sweet friend Jonadab,
Since Thamar is a virgin and my sister?

JONADAB

Thus it shall be: lie down upon thy bed,
Feigning thee fever-sick and ill-at-ease;
And when the king shall come to visit thee,
Desire thy sister Thamar may be sent
To dress some dainties for thy malady:
Then when thou hast her solely with thyself,
Enforce some favour to thy manly love.
See where she comes: entreat her in with thee.

[Enter **THAMAR**.

THAMAR

What aileth Amnon, with such sickly looks
To daunt the favour of his lovely face?

AMNON

Sweet Thamar, sick, and wish some wholesome cates
Dressed with the cunning of thy dainty hands.

THAMAR

That hath the king commanded at my hands;
Then come and rest thee, while I make thee ready
Some dainties easeful to thy crazèd soul.

AMNON

I go, sweet sister, easèd with thy sight.

[Exeunt **THAMAR**, **AMNON**, **JETHRAY**, and **PAGE**.

JONADAB

Why should a prince, whose power may command,
Obey the rebel passions of his love,
When they contend but 'gainst his consciënce,
And may be governed or suppressed by will? –
Now, Amnon, loose those loving knots of blood,
That sucked the courage from thy kingly heart,
And give it passage to thy withered cheeks.
Now, Thamar, ripened are the holy fruits
That grew on plants of thy virginity;
And rotten is thy name in Israel:
Poor Thamar, little did thy lovely hands
Foretell an action of such violence
As to contend with Amnon's lusty arms
Sinewed with vigour of his kindless love:
Fair Thamar, now dishonour hunts thy foot,
And follows thee through every covert shade,
Discovering thy shame and nakedness,
Even from the valleys of Jehosaphat
Up to the lofty mounts of Lebanon;
Where cedars, stirred with anger of the winds,
Sounding in storms the tale of thy disgrace,
Tremble with fury, and with murmur shake
Earth with their feet and with their heads the heavens,
Beating the clouds into their swiftest rack,
To bear this wonder round about the world.

[Exit.

SCENE IV

Outside the Door to Amnon's House.

Re-enter **AMNON** thrusting out **THAMAR**, and **JETHRAY**.

AMNON

Hence from my bed, whose sight offends my soul
As doth the parbreak of disgorgèd bears!

THAMAR

Unkind, unprincely, and unmanly Amnon,
To force, and then refuse thy sister's love,
Adding unto the fright of thy offence
The baneful torment of my published shame!
O, do not this dishonour to thy love,

Nor clog thy soul with such increasing sin!
This second evil far exceeds the first.

AMNON
Jethray, come thrust this woman from my sight,
And bolt the door upon her if she strive.

[Exit.

JETHRAY
Go, madam, go; away, you must begone;
My lord hath done with you: I pray, depart.

[Shuts her out. – Exit.

THAMAR
Whither, alas, ah, whither shall I fly,
With folded arms and all-amazèd soul?
Cast as was Eva from that glorious soil,
(Where all delights sat bating, winged with thoughts,
Ready to nestle in her naked breasts,)
To bare and barren vales with floods made waste,
To desert woods, and hills with lightening scorched,
With death, with shame, with hell, with horror sit;
There will I wander from my father's face;
There Absalon, my brother Absalon,
Sweet Absalon shall hear his sister mourn;
There will I lure with my windy sighs
Night-ravens and owls to rend my bloody side,
Which with a rusty weapon I will wound,
And make them passage to my panting heart.
Why talk'st thou, wretch, and leav'st the deed undone?
Rend hair and garments, as thy heart is rent
With inward fury of a thousand griefs,
And scatter them by these unhallowed doors,
To figure Amnon's resting cruëlty,
And tragic spoil of Thamar's chastity.

[Enter **ABSALON**.

ABSALON
What causeth Thamar to exclaim so much?

THAMAR
The cause that Thamar shameth to disclose.

ABSALON
Say; I thy brother will revenge that cause.

THAMAR
Amnon, our father's son, hath forcèd me,
And thrusts me from him as the scorn of Israel.

ABSALON
Hath Amnon forcèd thee? by David's hand,
And by the covenant God hath made with him,
Amnon shall bear his violence to hell;
Traitor to Heaven, traitor to David's throne,
Traitor to Absalon and Israel!
This fact hath Jacob's ruler seen from Heaven,
And through a cloud of smoke and tower of fire,
As he rides vaunting him upon the greens,
Shall tear his chariot-wheels with violent winds,
And throw his body in the bloody sea;
At him the thunder shall discharge his bolt;
And his fair spouse, with bright and fiery wings,
Sit ever burning on his hateful bones:
Myself, as swift as thunder or his spouse,
Will hunt occasion with a secret hate,
To work false Amnon an ungracious end. –
Go in, my sister; rest thee in my house;
And God in time shall take this shame from thee.

THAMAR
Nor God nor time will do that good for me.

[Exit.

SCENE V

Jerusalem.

Enter **DAVID** with his train.

DAVID
My Absalon, what mak'st thou here alone,
And bears such discontentment in thy brows?

ABSALON
Great cause hath Absalon to be displeased,
And in his heart to shroud the wounds of wrath.

DAVID
'Gainst whom should Absalon be thus displeased?

ABSALON

'Gainst wicked Amnon, thy ungracious son,
My brother and fair Thamar's by the king,
My step-brother by mother and by kind:
He hath dishonoured David's holiness,
And fixed a blot of lightness on his throne,
Forcing my sister Thamar when he feigned
A sickness, sprung from root of heinous lust.

DAVID

Hath Amnon brought this evil on my house,
And suffered sin to smite his father's bones?
Smite, David, deadlier than the voice of Heaven,
And let hate's fire be kindled in thy heart:
Frame in the arches of thy angry brows,
Making thy forehead, like a comet, shine,
To force false Amnon tremble at thy looks.
Sin, with his sevenfold crown and purple robe,
Begins his triumphs in my guilty throne;
There sits he watching with his hundred eyes
Our idle minutes and our wanton thoughts;
And with his baits, made of our frail desires,
Gives us the hook that hales our souls to hell:
But with the spirit of my kingdom's God
I'll thrust the flattering tyran from his throne,
And scourge his bondslaves from my hallowed court
With rods of iron and thorns of sharpened steel.
Then, Absalon, revenge not thou this sin;
Leave it to me, and I will chasten him.

ABSALON

I am content: then grant, my lord the king,
Himself with all his other lords would come
Up to my sheep-feast on the plain of Hazor.

DAVID

Nay, my fair son, myself with all my lords
Will bring thee too much charge; yet some shall go.

ABSALON

But let my lord the king himself take pains;
The time of year is pleasant for your grace,
And gladsome summer in her shady robes,
Crownèd with roses and with planted flowers,
With all her nymphs, shall entertain my lord,
That, from the thicket of my verdant groves,
Will sprinkle honey-dews about his breast,

And cast sweet balm upon his kingly head:
Then grant thy servant's boon, and go, my lord.

DAVID
Let it content my sweet son Absalon,
That I may stay, and take my other lords.

ABSALON
But shall thy best-belovèd Amnon go?

DAVID
What needeth it, that Amnon go with thee?

ABSALON
Yet do thy son and servant so much grace.

DAVID
Amnon shall go, and all my other lords,
Because I will give grace to Absalon.

[Enter **CUSAY** and **URIAS**, with **OTHERS**.

CUSAY
Pleaseth my lord the king, his servant Joab
Hath sent Urias from the Syrian wars.

DAVID
Welcome, Urias, from the Syrian wars,
Welcome to David as his dearest lord.

URIAS
Thanks be to Israel's God and David's grace,
Urias finds such greeting with the king.

DAVID
No other greeting shall Urias find
As long as David sways th' elected seat
And consecrated throne of Israel.
Tell me, Urias, of my servant Joab;
Fights he with truth the battles of our God,
And for the honour of the Lord's anointed?

URIAS
Thy servant Joab fights the chosen wars
With truth, with honour, and with high success,
And, 'gainst the wicked king of Ammon's sons,
Hath, by the finger of our sovereign's God,
Besieged the city Rabbah, and achieved

The court of waters, where the conduits run,
And all the Ammonites' delightsome springs:
Therefore he wisheth David's mightiness
Should number out the host of Israel,
And come in person to the city Rabbah,
That so her conquest may be made the king's,
And Joab fight as his inferior.

DAVID
This hath not God and Joab's prowess done
Without Urias' valours, I am sure,
Who, since his true conversion from a Hethite
To an adopted son of Israel,
Hath fought like one whose arms were lift by Heaven,
And whose bright sword was edged with Israel's wrath.
Go, therefore, home, Urias, take thy rest;
Visit thy wife and household with the joys
A victor and a favourite of the king's
Should exercise with honour after arms.

URIAS
Thy servant's bones are yet not half so crazed,
Nor constitute on such a sickly mould,
That for so little service he should faint,
And seek, as cowards, refuge of his home:
Nor are his thoughts so sensually stirred,
To stay the arms with which the Lord would smite
And fill their circle with his conquered foes,
For wanton bosom of a flattering wife.

DAVID
Urias hath a beauteous sober wife,
Yet young, and framed of tempting flesh and blood;
Then, when the king hath summoned thee from arms,
If thou unkindly shouldst refrain her bed,
Sin might be laid upon Urias' soul,
If Bethsabe by frailty hurt her fame:
Then go, Urias, solace in her love;
Whom God hath knit to thee, tremble to loose.

URIAS
The king is much too tender of my ease:
The ark and Israel and Judah dwell
In palaces and rich pavilions;
But Joab and his brother in the fields,
Suffering the wrath of winter and the sun:
And shall Urias (of more shame than they)
Banquet, and loiter in the work of Heaven?

As sure as thy soul doth live, my lord,
Mine ears shall never lean to such delight,
When holy labour calls me forth to fight.

DAVID
Then be it with Urias' manly heart
As best his fame may shine in Israel.

URIAS
Thus shall Urias' heart be best content,
Till thou dismiss me back to Joab's bands:
This ground before the king my master's doors
Shall be my couch, and this unwearied arm
The proper pillow of a soldier's head;

[Lies down.

For never will I lodge within my house,
Till Joab triumph in my secret vows.

DAVID
Then fetch some flagons of our purest wine,
That we may welcome home our hardy friend
With full carouses to his fortunes past
And to the honours of his future arms;
Then will I send him back to Rabbah siege,
And follow with the strength of Israel.

[Enter one with flagons of wine.

Arise, Urias; come and pledge the king.

URIAS
If David think me worthy such a grace,
I will be bold and pledge my lord the king.

[Rises.

DAVID
Absalon and Cusay both shall drink
To good Urias and his happiness.

ABSALON
We will, my lord, to please Urias' soul.

DAVID
I will begin, Urias, to thyself,
And all the treasure of the Ammonites,

Which here I promise to impart to thee,
And bind that promise with a full carouse.

[Drinks.

URIAS
What seemeth pleasant in my sovereign's eyes,
That shall Urias do till he be dead.

DAVID
Fill him the cup. –

[**URIAS** drinks.

Follow, ye lords that love
Your sovereign's health, and do as he hath done.

ABSALON
Ill may he thrive, or live in Israel,
That loves not David, or denies his charge. –
Urias, here is to Abisai's health,
Lord Joab's brother and thy loving friend.

[Drinks.

URIAS
I pledge Lord Absalon and Abisai's health.

[Drinks.

CUSAY
Here now, Urias, to the health of Joab,
And to the pleasant journey we shall have
When we return to mighty Rabbah siege.

[Drinks.

URIAS
Cusay, I pledge thee all with all my heart. –
Give me some drink, ye servants of the king;
Give me my drink.

[Drinks.

DAVID
Well done, my good Urias! drink thy fill,
That in thy fulness David may rejoice.

URIAS
I will, my lord.

ABSALON
Now, Lord Urias, one carouse to me.

URIAS
No, sir, I'll drink to the king;
Your father is a better man than you.

DAVID
Do so, Urias; I will pledge thee straight.

URIAS
I will indeed, my lord and sovereign;
I'll once in my days be so bold.

DAVID
Fill him his glass.

URIAS
Fill me my glass.
He gives him the glass.

DAVID
Quickly, I say.

URIAS
Quickly, I say. – Here, my lord, by your favour now I drink to you.

[Drinks.

DAVID
I pledge thee, good Urias, presently.

[Drinks.

ABSALON
Here, then, Urias, once again for me,
And to the health of David's children.

[Drinks.

URIAS
David's children!

ABSALON

Ay, David's children: wilt thou pledge me, man?

URIAS
Pledge me, man!

ABSALON
Pledge me, I say, or else thou lov'st us not.

URIAS
What, do you talk? do you talk? I'll no more; I'll lie down here.

DAVID
Rather, Urias, go thou home and sleep.

URIAS
O, ho, sir! would you make me break my sentence?

[Lies down.

Home, sir! no, indeed, sir: I'll sleep upon mine arm, like a soldier; sleep like a man as long as I live in Israel.

DAVID [Aside]
If naught will serve to save his wife's renown,
I'll send him with a letter unto Joab
To put him in the forefront of the wars,
That so my purposes may take effect. –
Help him in, sirs.

[Exeunt **DAVID** and **ABSALON**.

CUSAY
Come, rise, Urias; get thee in and sleep.

URIAS
I will not go home, sir; that's flat.

CUSAY
Then come and rest thee upon David's bed.

URIAS
On, afore, my lords, on, afore.

[Exeunt.

CHORUS I.

[Enter **CHORUS**.

CHORUS
O proud revolt of a presumptuous man,
Laying his bridle in the neck of sin,
Ready to bear him past his grave to hell!
Like as the fatal raven, that in his voice
Carries the dreadful summons of our deaths,
Flies by the fair Arabian spiceries,
Her pleasant gardens and delightsome parks,
Seeming to curse them with his hoarse exclaims,
And yet doth stoop with hungry violence
Upon a piece of hateful carrion;
So wretched man, displeased with those delights
Would yield a quickening savour to his soul,
Pursues with eager and unstanchèd thirst
The greedy longings of his loathsome flesh.
If holy David so shook hands with sin,
What shall our baser spirits glory in?
This kingly giving lust her rein
Pursues the sequel with a greater ill.
Urias in the forefront of the wars
Is murthered by the hateful heathens' sword,
And David joys his too dear Bethsabe.
Suppose this past, and that the child is born,
Whose death the prophet solemnly doth mourn.

[Exit.

SCENE VI

The Royal Palace at Jerusalem.

Enter **BETHSABE** with her **HANDMAID**.

BETHSABE
Mourn, Bethsabe, bewail thy foolishness,
Thy sin, thy shame, the sorrow of thy soul:
Sin, shame, and sorrow swarm about thy soul;
And, in the gates and entrance of my heart,
Sadness, with wreathèd arms, hangs her complaint.
No comfort from the ten-stringed instrument,
The twinkling cymbal, or the ivory lute;
Nor doth the sound of David's kingly harp
Make glad the broken heart of Bethsabe:

Jerusalem is filled with thy complaint,
And in the streets of Sion sits thy grief.
The babe is sick, sick to the death, I fear,
The fruit that sprung from thee to David's house;
Nor may the pot of honey and of oil
Glad David or his handmaid's countenance.
Urias – wo is me to think hereon!
For who is it among the sons of men
That saith not to my soul, "The king hath sinned;
David hath done amiss, and Bethsabe
Laid snares of death unto Urias' life"?
My sweet Urias, fall'n into the pit
Art thou, and gone even to the gates of hell
For Bethsabe, that wouldst not shroud her shame.
O, what is it to serve the lust of kings!
How lion-like th[e]y rage when we resist!
But, Bethsabe, in humbleness attend
The grace that God will to his handmaid send.

[Exeunt.

SCENE VII

The Palace.

Enter **DAVID** in his gown, walking sadly;

SERVANTS attending.

DAVID [Aside]
The babe is sick, and sad is David's heart,
To see the guiltless bear the guilty's pain.
David, hang up thy harp; hang down thy head;
And dash thy ivory lute against the stones.
The dew, that on the hill of Hermon falls,
Rains not on Sion's tops and lofty towers;
The plains of Gath and Askaron rejoice,
And David's thoughts are spent in pensiveness:
The babe is sick, sweet babe, that Bethsabe
With woman's pain brought forth to Israel.

[Enter **NATHAN**.

But what saith Nathan to his lord the king?

NATHAN

Thus Nathan saith unto his lord the king:
There were two men both dwellers in one town;
The one was mighty, and exceeding rich
In oxen, sheep, and cattle of the field;
The other poor, having nor ox, nor calf,
Nor other cattle, save one little lamb
Which he had bought and nourished by the hand;
And it grew up, and fed with him and his,
And eat and drank as he and his were wont,
And in his bosom slept, and was to live
As was his daughter or his dearest child.
There came a stranger to this wealthy man;
And he refused and spared to take his own,
Or of his store to dress or make him meat,
But took the poor man's sheep, partly, poor man's store,
And dressed it for this stranger in his house.
What, tell me, shall be done to him for this?

DAVID
Now, as the Lord doth live, this wicked man
Is judged and shall become the child of death;
Fourfold to the poor man shall he restore,
That without mercy took his lamb away.

NATHAN
Thou art the man; and thou hast judged thyself.
David, thus saith the Lord thy God by me:
"I thee anointed king in Israel,
And saved thee from the tyranny of Saul;
Thy master's house I gave thee to possess;
His wives into thy bosom did I give,
And Judah and Jerusalem withal;
And might, thou know'st, if this had been too small,
Have given thee more:
Wherefore, then, hast thou gone so far astray,
And hast done evil, and sinned in my sight?
Urias thou hast killèd with the sword;
Yea, with the sword of the uncircumcised
Thou hast him slain: wherefore, from this day forth,
The sword shall never go from thee and thine;
For thou hast ta'en this Hethite's wife to thee:
Wherefore, behold, I will," saith Jacob's God,
"In thine own house stir evil up to thee;
Yea, I before thy face will take thy wives,
And give them to thy neighbour to possess:
This shall be done to David in the day,
That Israel openly may see thy shame."

DAVID
Nathan, I have against the Lord, I have
Sinnèd; O, sinnèd grievously! and, lo,
From Heaven's throne doth David throw himself,
And groan and grovel to the gates of hell!

[Falls down.

NATHAN [Raising him]
David, stand up: thus saith the Lord by me:
David the king shall live, for He hath seen
The true repentant sorrow of thy heart;
But, for thou hast in this misdeed of thine
Stirred up the enemies of Israel
To triumph, and blaspheme the God of Hosts,
And say, he set a wicked man to reign
Over his lovèd people and his tribes, –
The child shall surely die, that erst was born,
His mother's sin, his kingly father's scorn.

[Exit.

DAVID
How just is Jacob's God in all his works!
But must it die that David loveth so?
O, that the Mighty One of Israel
Nill change his doom, and says the babe must die!
Mourn, Israel, and weep in Sion-gates;
Wither, ye cedar-trees of Lebanon;
Ye sprouting almonds, with your flowering tops,
Droop, drown, and drench in Hebron's fearful streams:
The babe must die that was to David born,
His mother's sin, his kingly father's scorn.

[Sits sadly.

[Enter **CUSAY**.

1st SERVANT
What tidings bringeth Cusay to the king?

CUSAY
To thee, the servant of King David's court,
This bringeth Cusay, as the prophet spake;
The Lord hath surely stricken to the death
The child new-born by that Urias' wife,
That by the sons of Ammon erst was slain.

1st SERVANT
Cusay, be still; the king is vexèd sore:
How shall he speed that brings this tidings first,
When, while the child was yet alive, we spake,
And David's heart would not be comforted?

DAVID
Yea, David's heart will not be comforted!
What murmur ye, the servants of the king?
What tidings telleth Cusay to the king?
Say, Cusay, lives the child, or is he dead?

CUSAY
The child is dead, that of Urias' wife
David begat.

DAVID
rias' wife, saist thou?
The child is dead, then ceaseth David's shame:
Fetch me to eat, and give me wine to drink;
Water to wash, and oil to clear my looks;
Bring down your shalms, your cymbals, and your pipes;
Let David's harp and lute, his hand and voice,
Give laud to him that loveth Israel,
And sing his praise that shendeth David's fame,
That put away his sin from out his sight,
And sent his shame into the streets of Gath.
Bring ye to me the mother of the babe,
That I may wipe the tears from off her face,
And give her comfort with this hand of mine,
And deck fair Bethsabe with ornaments,
That she may bear to me another son,
That may be lovèd of the Lord of Hosts;
For where he is, of force must David go,
But never may he come where David is.

[They bring in water, wine, and oil.

[Music and a banquet; and enter **BETHSABE**.

Fair Bethsabe, sit thou, and sigh no more: –
And sing and play, you servants of the king:
Now sleepeth David's sorrow with the dead,
And Bethsabe liveth to Israel.

[They use all solemnities together and sing, etc.

Now arms and warlike engines for assault

Prepare at once, ye men of Israel,
Ye men of Judah and Jerusalem,
That Rabbah may be taken by the king,
Lest it be callèd after Joab's name,
Nor David's glory shine in Sion streets.
To Rabbah marcheth David with his men,
To chastise Ammon and the wicked ones.

[Exeunt.

SCENE VIII

A Field.

Enter **ABSALON** with several **OTHERS**.

ABSALON
Set up your mules, and give them well to eat,
And let us meet our brothers at the feast.
Accursèd is the master of this feast,
Dishonour of the house of Israel,
His sister's slander, and his mother's shame:
Shame be his share that could such ill contrive,
To ravish Thamar, and, without a pause,
To drive her shamefully from out his house:
But may his wickedness find just reward!
Therefore doth Absalon conspire with you,
That Amnon die what time he sits to eat;
For in the holy temple have I sworn
Wreak of his villany in Thamar's rape.
And here he comes: bespeak him gently, all,
Whose death is deeply gravèd in my heart.

[Enter **AMNON, ADONIA**, and **JONADAB**.

AMNON
Our shearers are not far from hence, I wot;
And Amnon to you all his brethren
Giveth such welcome as our fathers erst
Were wont in Judah and Jerusalem; –
But, specially, Lord Absalon, to thee,
The honour of thy house and progeny:
Sit down and dine with me, King David's son,
Thou fair young man, whose hairs shine in mine eye
Like golden wires of David's ivory lute.

ABSALON
Amnon, where be thy shearers and thy men,
That we may pour in plenty of thy vines,
And eat thy goats'-milk, and rejoice with thee?

AMNON
Here cometh Amnon's shearers and his men: –
Absalon, sit and rejoice with me.

[Enter a company of **SHEPHERDS**, who dance and sing.

Drink, Absalon, in praise of Israel;
Welcome to Amnon's fields from David's court.

ABSALON [Stabbing **AMNON**]
Die with thy draught; perish, and die accursed;
Dishonour to the honour of us all;
Die for the villany to Thamar done,
Unworthy thou to be King David's son!

[Exit with **OTHERS**.

JONADAB
O, what hath Absalon for Thamar done,
Murthered his brother, great King David's son!

ADONIA
Run, Jonadab, away, and make it known,
What cruèlty this Absalon hath shown. –
Amnon, thy brother Ádonia shall
Bury thy body 'mong the dead men's bones;
And we will make complaint to Israel
Of Amnon's death and pride of Absalon.

[Exeunt.

SCENE IX

Rabbah, Outside the City's Walls.

Enter **DAVID**, **JOAB**, **ABISAI**, **CUSAY**, and **OTHERS**, with drum and ensign against Rabbah.

DAVID
This is the town of the uncircumcised,
The city of the kingdom, this is it,
Rabbah, where wicked Hanon sitteth king.

Despoil this king, this Hanon of his crown;
Unpeople Rabbah and the streets thereof;
For in their blood, and slaughter of the slain,
Lieth the honour of King David's line.
Joab, Abisai, and the rest of you,
Fight ye this day for great Jerusalem.

[Enter **HANON** and **OTHERS** on the walls.

JOAB
And see where Hanon shows him on the walls;
Why, then, do we forbear to give assault,
That Israel may, as it is promisèd,
Subdue the daughters of the Gentiles' tribes?
All this must be performed by David's hand.

DAVID
Hark to me, Hanon, and remember well:
As sure as He doth live that kept my host,
What time our young men, by the pool of Gibeon,
Went forth against the strength of Isboseth,
And twelve to twelve did with their weapons play;
So sure art thou and thy men of war
To feel the sword of Israel this day,
Because thou hast defièd Jacob's God,
And suffered Rabbah with the Philistine
To rail upon the tribe of Benjamin.

HANON
Hark, man: as sure as Saul thy master fell,
And gored his sides upon the mountain-tops,
And Jonathan, Abinadab, and Melchisua,
Watered the dales and deeps of Askaron
With bloody streams, that from Gilboa ran
In channels through the wilderness of Ziph,
What time the sword of the uncircumcised
Was drunken with the blood of Israel;
So sure shall David perish with his men
Under the walls of Rabbah, Hanon's town.

JOAB
Hanon, the God of Israel hath said,
David the king shall wear that crown of thine
That weighs a talent of the finest gold,
And triumph in the spoil of Hanon's town,
When Israel shall hale thy people hence,
And turn them to the tile-kiln, man and child,
And put them under harrows made of iron,

And hew their bones with axes, and their limbs
With iron swords divide and tear in twain.
Hanon, this shall be done to thee and thine,
Because thou hast defièd Israel. –
To arms, to arms, that Rabbah feel revenge,
And Hanon's town become King David's spoil!

[Alarum, excursions, assault; exeunt.

[Then the trumpets sound, and re-enter **DAVID** with Hanon's crown, **JOAB**, etc.

DAVID
Now clattering arms and wrathful storms of war
Have thundered over Rabbah's razèd towers;
The wreakful ire of great Jehovah's arm,
That for his people made the gates to rend,
And clothed the cherubins in fiery coats
To fight against the wicked Hanon's town.
Pay thanks, ye men of Judah, to the King,
The God of Sion and Jerusalem,
That hath exalted Israel to this,
And crownèd David with this diadem.

JOAB
Beauteous and bright is he among the tribes;
As when the sun, attired in glistering robe,
Comes dancing from his oriental gate,
And bridegroom-like hurls through the gloomy air
His radiant beams, such doth King David show,
Crowned with the honour of his enemies' town,
Shining in riches like the firmament,
The starry vault that overhangs the earth:
So looketh David King of Israel.

ABISAI
Joab, why doth not David mount his throne
Whom Heaven hath beautified with Hanon's crown?
Sound trumpets, shalms, and instruments of praise,
To Jacob's God for David's victory.

[Trumpets, etc.

[Enter **JONADAB**.

JONADAB
Why doth the King of Israel rejoice?
Why sitteth David crowned with Rabbah's rule?
Behold, there hath great heaviness befall'n

In Amnon's fields by Absalon's misdeed;
And Amnon's shearers and their feast of mirth
Absalon hath o'erturnèd with his sword;
Nor liveth any of King David's sons
To bring this bitter tidings to the king.

DAVID

Ay me, how soon are David's triumphs dashed,
How suddenly declineth David's pride!
As doth the daylight settle in the west,
So dim is David's glory and his gite.
Die, David; for to thee is left no seed
That may revive thy name in Israel.

JONADAB

In Israel is left of David's seed. –
Comfort your lord, you servants of the king. –
Behold, thy sons return in mourning weeds,
And only Amnon Absalon hath slain.

[Enter **ADONIA** with other **SONS** of David.

DAVID

Welcome, my sons; dearer to me you are
Than is this golden crown or Hanon's spoil.
O, tell me, then, tell me, my sons, I say,
How cometh it to pass that Absalon
Hath slain his brother Amnon with the sword?

ADONIA

Thy sons, O king, went up to Amnon's fields,
To feast with him and eat his bread and oil;
And Absalon upon his mule doth come,
And to his men he saith, "When Amnon's heart
Is merry and secure, then strike him dead,
Because he forcèd Thamar shamefully,
And hated her, and threw her forth his doors."
And this did he; and they with him conspire,
And kill thy son in wreak of Thamar's wrong.

DAVID

How long shall Judah and Jerusalem
Complain, and water Sion with their tears!
How long shall Israel lament in vain,
And not a man among the mighty ones
Will hear the sorrows of King David's heart!
Amnon, thy life was pleasing to thy lord,
As to mine ears the music of my lute,

Or songs that David tuneth to his harp;
And Absalon hath ta'en from me away
The gladness of my sad distressèd soul.

[Exeunt **JOAB** and some **OTHERS.**

[Enter **WOMAN** of Thecoa.

WOMAN [Kneeling]
God save King David, King of Israel,
And bless the gates of Sion for his sake!

DAVID
Woman, why mournest thou? rise from the earth;
Tell me what sorrow hath befall'n thy soul.

WOMAN [Rising]
Thy servant's soul, O king, is troubled sore,
And grievous is the anguish of her heart;
And from Thecoa doth thy handmaid come.

DAVID
Tell me, and say, thou Woman of Thecoa,
What aileth thee or what is come to pass.

WOMAN
Thy servant is a widow in Thecoa.
Two sons thy handmaid had; and they, my lord,
Fought in the field, where no man went betwixt,
And so the one did smite and slay the other.
And, lo, behold, the kindred doth arise,
And cry on him that smote his brother,
That he therefóre may be the child of death;
"For we will follow and destroy the heir."
So will they quench that sparkle that is left,
And leave nor name nor issue on the earth
To me or to thy handmaid's husband dead.

DAVID
Woman, return; go home unto thy house:
I will take order that thy son be safe.
If any man say otherwise than well,
Bring him to me, and I shall chastise him;
For, as the Lord doth live, shall not a hair
Shed from thy son or fall upon the earth.
Woman, to God alone belongs revenge:
Shall, then, the kindred slay him for his sin?

WOMAN

Well hath King David to his handmaid spoke:
But wherefore, then, hast thou determinèd
So hard a part against the righteous tribes,
To follow and pursue the banishèd,
Whenas to God alone belongs revenge?
Assuredly thou saist against thyself:
Therefore call home again the banishèd;
Call home the banishèd, that he may live,
And raise to thee some fruit in Israel.

DAVID

Thou woman of Thecoa, answer me,
Answer me one thing I shall ask of thee:
Is not the hand of Joab in this work?
Tell me, is not his finger in this fact?

WOMAN

It is, my lord; his hand is in this work:
Assure thee, Joab, captain of thy host,
Hath put these words into thy handmaid's mouth;
And thou art as an angel from on high,
To understand the meaning of my heart:
Lo, where he cometh to his lord the king.

[Re-enter **JOAB**.

DAVID

Say, Joab, didst thou send this woman in
To put this parable for Absalon?

JOAB

Joab, my lord, did bid this woman speak,
And she hath said; and thou hast understood.

DAVID

I have, and am content to do the thing.
Go fetch my son, that he may live with me.

JOAB [Kneeling]

Now God be blessèd for King David's life!
Thy servant Joab hath found grace with thee,
In that thou sparest Absalon thy child.

[Rises.

A beautiful and fair young man is he,
In all his body is no blemish seen;

His hair is like the wire of David's harp,
That twines about his bright and ivory neck;
In Israel is not such a goodly man;
And here I bring him to entreat for grace.

[JOAB brings in ABSALON.

DAVID
Hast thou slain Amnon in the fields of Hazor –
Ah, Absalon, my son I ah, my son, Absalon!
But wherefore do I vex thy spirit so?
Live, and return from Gesur to thy house;
Return from Gesur to Jerusalem:
What boots it to be bitter to thy soul?
Amnon is dead, and Absalon survives.

ABSALON
Father, I have offended Israel,
I have offended David and his house;
For Thamar's wrong hath Absalon misdone:
But David's heart is free from sharp revenge,
And Joab hath got grace for Absalon.

DAVID
Depart with me, you men of Israel,
You that have followed Rabbah with the sword,
And ransack Ammon's richest treasuries. –
Live, Absalon, my son, live once in peace:
Peace be with thee, and with Jerusalem!

[Exeunt ALL except ABSALON.

ABSALON
David is gone, and Absalon remains,
Flowering in pleasant spring-time of his youth:
Why liveth Absalon and is not honoured
Of tribes and elders and the mightiest ones,
That round about his temples he may wear
Garlands and wreaths set on with reverence;
That every one that hath a cause to plead
Might come to Absalon and call for right?
Then in the gates of Sion would I sit,
And publish laws in great Jerusalem;
And not a man should live in all the land
But Absalon would do him reason's due:
Therefore I shall address me, as I may,
To love the men and tribes of Israel.

[Exit.

The Mount of Olives.

Enter **DAVID**, **ITHAY**, **SADOC**, **AHIMAAS**, **JONATHAN**, and **OTHERS**; **DAVID** barefoot, with some loose covering over his head; and all mourning.

DAVID
Proud lust, the bloodiest traitor to our souls,
Whose greedy throat nor earth, air, sea, or Heaven,
Can glut or satisfy with any store,
Thou art the cause these torments suck my blood,
Piercing with venom of thy poisoned eyes
The strength and marrow of my tainted bones.
To punish Pharaoh and his cursèd host,
The waters shrunk at great Adonai's voice
And sandy bottom of the sea appeared,
Offering his service at his servant's feet;
And, to inflict a plague on David's sin,
He makes his bowels traitors to his breast,
Winding about his heart with mortal gripes. –
Ah, Absalon, the wrath of Heaven inflames
Thy scorchèd bosom with ambitious heat,
And Satan sets thee on a lusty tower,
Showing thy thoughts the pride of Israel,
Of choice to cast thee on her ruthless stones! –
Weep with me, then, ye sons of Israel;
Lie down with David, and with David mourn
Before the Holy One that sees our hearts;

[Lies down, and all the rest after him.

Season this heavy soil with showers of tears,
And fill the face of every flower with dew;
Weep, Israel, for David's soul dissolves,
Lading the fountains of his drownèd eyes,
And pours her substance on the senseless earth.

SADOC
Weep, Israel; O, weep for David's soul,
Strewing the ground with hair and garments torn,
For tragic witness of your hearty woes!

AHIMAAS

O, would our eyes were conduits to our hearts,
And that our hearts were seas of liquid blood,
To pour in streams upon this holy mount,
For witness we would die for David's woes!

JONATHAN
Then should this Mount of Olives seem a plain
Drowned with a sea, that with our sighs should roar,
And, in the murmur of his mounting waves,
Report our bleeding sorrows to the heavens,
For witness we would die for David's woes.

ITHAY
Earth cannot weep enough for David's woes:
Then weep, you heavens, and, all you clouds, dissolve,
That piteous stars may see our miseries,
And drop their golden tears upon the ground,
For witness how they weep for David's woes.

SADOC
Now let my sovereign raise his prostrate bones,
And mourn not as a faithless man would do;
But be assured that Jacob's righteous God,
That promised never to forsake your throne,
Will still be just and pure in his vows.

DAVID
Sadoc, high-priest, preserver of the ark,
Whose sacred virtue keeps the chosen crown,
I know my God is spotless in his vows,
And that these hairs shall greet my grave in peace:
But that my son should wrong his tendered soul,
And fight against his father's happiness,
Turns all my hopes into despair of him,
And that despair feeds all my veins with grief.

ITHAY
Think of it, David, as a fatal plague
Which grief preserveth, but preventeth not;
And turn thy drooping eyes upon the troops
That, of affection to thy worthiness,
Do swarm about the person of the king:
Cherish their valours and their zealous loves
With pleasant looks and sweet encouragements.

DAVID
Methinks the voice of Ithay fills mine ears.

ITHAY

Let not the voice of Ithay loathe thine ears,
Whose heart would balm thy bosom with his tears.

DAVID

But wherefore go'st thou to the wars with us?
Thou art a stranger here in Israel,
And son to Achis, mighty King of Gath;
Therefore return, and with thy father stay:
Thou cam'st but yesterday; and should I now
Let thee partake these troubles here with us?
Keep both thyself and all thy soldiers safe:
Let me abide the hazards of these arms,
And God requite the friendship thou hast showed.

ITHAY

As sure as Israel's God gives David life,
What place or peril shall contain the king,
The same will Ithay share in life and death.

DAVID

Then, gentle Ithay, be thou still with us,
A joy to David, and a grace to Israel. –
Go, Sadoc, now, and bear the ark of God
Into the great Jerusalem again:
If I find favour in his gracious eyes,
Then will he lay his hand upon my heart
Yet once again before I visit death;
Giving it strength, and virtue to mine eyes,
To taste the comforts and behold the form
Of his fair ark and holy tabernacle:
But, if he say, "My wonted love is worn,
And I have no delight in David now,"
Here lie I armèd with an humble heart
T' embrace the pains that anger shall impose,
And kiss the sword my lord shall kill me with.
Then, Sadoc, take Ahimaäs thy son,
With Jonathan son to Abiathar;
And in these fields will I repose myself,
Till they return from you some certain news.

SADOC

Thy servants will with joy obey the king,
And hope to cheer his heart with happy news.

[Exeunt **SADOC**, **AHIMAAS**, and **JONATHAN**.

ITHAY

Now that it be no grief unto the king,
Let me for good inform his majesty,
That, with unkind and graceless Absalon,
Achitophel your ancient counsellor
Directs the state of this rebellion.

DAVID
Then doth it aim with danger at my crown. –

[Kneeling.

O thou, that hold'st his raging bloody bound
Within the circle of the silver moon,
That girds earth's centre with his watery scarf,
Limit the counsel of Achitophel,
No bounds extending to my soul's distress,
But turn his wisdom into foolishness!

[Enter **CUSAY** with his coat turned and head covered.

CUSAY
Happiness and honour to my lord the king!

DAVID
What happiness or honour may betide
His state that toils in my extremities?

CUSAY
O, let my gracious sovereign cease these griefs,
Unless he wish his servant Cusay's death,
Whose life depends upon my lord's relief!
Then let my presence with my sighs perfume
The pleasant closet of my sovereign's soul.

DAVID
No, Cusay, no; thy presence unto me
Will be a burden, since I tender thee,
And cannot break thy sighs for David's sake:
But if thou turn to fair Jerusalem,
And say to Absalon, as thou hast been
A trusty friend unto his father's seat,
So thou wilt be to him, and call him king,
Achitophel's counsel may be brought to naught.
Then having Sadoc and Abiathar,
All three may learn the secrets of my son,
Sending the message by Ahimaäs,
And friendly Jonathan, who both are there.

CUSAY
Then rise, referring the success to Heaven.

DAVID
Cusay, I rise; though with unwieldy bones
I carry arms against my Absalon.

[Exeunt.

The Palace in Jerusalem.

ABSALON, AMASA, ACHITOPHEL, with the **CONCUBINES** of David, and others, are discovered in great state; **ABSALON** crowned.

ABSALON
Now you that were my father's concubines,
Liquor to his inchaste and lustful fire,
Have seen his honour shaken in his house,
Which I possess in sight of all the world;
I bring ye forth for foils to my renown,
And to eclipse the glory of your king,
Whose life is with his honour fast enclosed
Within the entrails of a jetty cloud,
Whose dissolution shall pour down in showers
The substance of his life and swelling pride:
Then shall the stars light earth with rich aspécts,
And Heaven shall burn in love with Absalon,
Whose beauty will suffice to chase all mists,
And clothe the sun's sphere with a triple fire,
Sooner than his clear eyes should suffer stain,
Or be offended with a lowering day.

1st CONCUBINE
Thy father's honour, graceless Absalon,
And ours thus beaten with thy violent arms,
Will cry for vengeance to the host of Heaven,
Whose power is ever armed against the proud,
And will dart plagues at thy aspiring head
For doing this disgrace to David's throne.

2nd CONCUBINE
To David's throne, to David's holy throne,
Whose sceptre angels guard with swords of fire,
And sit as eagles on his conquering fist,

Ready to prey upon his enemies:
Then think not thou, the captain of his foes,
Wert thou much swifter than Azahell was,
That could outpace the nimble-footed roe,
To scape the fury of their thumping beaks
Or dreadful scope of their commanding wings.

ACHITOPHEL
Let not my lord the King of Israel
Be angry with a silly woman's threats;
But, with the pleasure he hath erst enjoyed,
Turn them into their cabinets again,
Till David's conquest be their overthrow.

ABSALON
Into your bowers, ye daughters of disdain,
Gotten by fury of unbridled lust,
And wash your couches with your mourning tears,
For grief that David's kingdom is decayed.

1st CONCUBINE
No, Absalon, his kingdom is enchained
Fast to the finger of great Jacob's God,
Which will not loose it for a rebel's love.

[Exeunt **CONCUBINES**.

AMASA
If I might give advice unto the king,
These concubines should buy their taunts with blood.

ABSALON
Amasa, no; but let thy martial sword
Empty the veins of David's armèd men,
And let these foolish women scape our hands
To recompense the shame they have sustained.
First, Absalon was by the trumpet's sound
Proclaimed through Hebron King of Israel;
And now is set in fair Jerusalem
With cómplete state and glory of a crown:
Fifty fair footmen by my chariot run,
And to the air whose rupture rings my fame,
Where'er I ride, they offer reverence.
Why should not Absalon, that in his face
Carries the final purpose of his God,
That is, to work him grace in Israel,
Endeavour to achieve with all his strength
The state that most may satisfy his joy,

Keeping his statutes and his covenants pure?
His thunder is entangled in my hair,
And with my beauty is his lightning quenched:
I am the man he made to glory in,
When by the errors of my father's sin
He lost the path that led into the land
Wherewith our chosen ancestors were blessed.

[Enter **CUSAY**.

CUSAY
Long may the beauteous King of Israel live,
To whom the people do by thousands swarm!

ABSALON
What meaneth Cusay so to greet his foe?
Is this the love thou shewdst to David's soul,
To whose assistance thou hast vowed thy life?
Why leav'st thou him in this extremity?

CUSAY
Because the Lord and Israel chooseth thee;
And as before I served thy father's turn
With counsel ácceptable in his sight,
So likewise will I now obey his son.

ABSALON
Then welcome, Cusay, to King Absalon. –
And now, my lords and loving counsellors,
I think it time to exercise our arms
Against forsaken David and his host.
Give counsel first, my good Achitophel,
What times and orders we may best observe
For prosperous manage of these high exploits.

ACHITOPHEL
Let me choose out twelve thousand valiant men:
And, while the night hides with her sable mists
The close endeavours cunning soldiers use,
I will assault thy discontented sire;
And, while with weakness of their weary arms,
Surcharged with toil, to shun thy sudden power,
The people fly in huge disordered troops
To save their lives, and leave the king alone,
Then will I smite him with his latest wound,
And bring the people to thy feet in peace.

ABSALON

Well hath Achitophel given his advice.
Yet let us hear what Cusay counsels us,
Whose great experience is well worth the ear.

CUSAY
Though wise Achitophel be much more meet
To purchase hearing with my lord the king,
For all his former counsels, than myself,
Yet, not offending Absalon or him,
This time it is not good nor worth pursuit;
For, well thou know'st, thy father's men are strong,
Chafing as she-bears robbèd of their whelps:
Besides, the king himself a valiant man,
Trained up in feats and stratagems of war;
And will not, for prevention of the worst,
Lodge with the common soldiers in the field;
But now, I know, his wonted policies
Have taught him lurk within some secret cave,
Guarded with all his stoutest soldiers;
Which, if the forefront of his battle faint,
Will yet give out that Absalon doth fly,
And so thy soldiers be discouragèd:
David himself withal, whose angry heart
Is as a lion's letted of his walk,
Will fight himself, and all his men to one,
Before a few shall vanquish him by fear.
My counsel therefore is, with trumpet's sound
To gather men from Dan to Bersabe,
That they may march in number like sea-sands,
That nestle close in one another's neck:
So shall we come upon him in our strength,
Like to the dew that falls in showers from Heaven,
And leave him not a man to march withal.
Besides, if any city succour him,
The numbers of our men shall fetch us ropes,
And we will pull it down the river's stream,
That not a stone be left to keep us out.

ABSALON
What says my lord to Cusay's counsel now?

AMASA
I fancy Cusay's counsel better far
Than that is given us from Achitophel;
And so, I think, doth every soldier here.

ALL
Cusay's counsel is better than Achitophel's.

ABSALON
Then march we after Cusay's counsel all:
Sound trumpets through the bounds of Israel,
And muster all the men will serve the king,
That Absalon may glut his longing soul
With sole fruition of his father's crown.

ACHITOPHEL [Aside]
Ill shall they fare that follow thy attempts,
That scorns the counsel of Achitophel.

[Exeunt all except **CUSAY**.

CUSAY
Thus hath the power of Jacob's jealous God
Fulfilled his servant David's drifts by me,
And brought Achitophel's advice to scorn.

[Enter **SADOC**, **ABIATHAR**, **AHIMAAS**, and **JONATHAN**.

SADOC
God save Lord Cusay, and direct his zeal
To purchase David's conquest 'gainst his son!

ABIATHAR
What secrets hast thou gleaned from Absalon?

CUSAY
These, sacred priests that bear the ark of God: –
Achitophel advised him in the night
To let him choose twelve thousand fighting men,
And he would come on David at unwares,
While he was weary with his violent toil:
But I advised to get a greater host,
And gather men from Dan to Bersabe,
To come upon him strongly in the fields.
Then send Ahimaäs and Jonathan
To signify these secrets to the king,
And will him not to stay this night abroad;
But get him over Jordan presently,
Lest he and all his people kiss the sword.

SADOC
Then go, Ahimaäs and Jonathan,
And straight convey this message to the king.

AHIMAAS

Father, we will, if Absalon's chief spies
Prevent not this device, and stay us here.

[Exeunt.

SCENE XII

The Road Near the Village of Bahurim.

Enter **SEMEI**.

SEMEI
The man of Israel that hath ruled as king,
Or rather as the tyrant of the land,
Bolstering his hateful head upon the throne
That God unworthily hath blessed him with,
Shall now, I hope, lay it as low as hell,
And be deposed from his detested chair.
O, that my bosom could by nature bear
A sea of poison, to be poured upon
His cursèd head that sacred balm hath graced
And consecrated King of Israel!
Or would my breath were made the smoke of hell,
Infected with the sighs of damnèd souls,
Or with the reeking of that serpent's gorge
That feeds on adders, toads, and venomous roots,
That, as I opened my revenging lips
To curse the shepherd for his tyranny,
My words might cast rank poison to his pores,
And make his swoln and rankling sinews crack,
Like to the combat-blows that break the clouds
When Jove's stout champions fight with fire.
See where he cometh that my soul abhors!
I have prepared my pocket full of stones
To cast at him, mingled with earth and dust,
Which, bursting with disdain, I greet him with. –

[Enter **DAVID, JOAB, ABISAI, ITHAY,** and **OTHERS.**

Come forth, thou murtherer and wicked man:
The lord hath brought upon thy cursèd head
The guiltless blood of Saul and all his sons,
Whose royal throne thy baseness hath usurped;
And, to revenge it deeply on thy soul,
The Lord hath given the kingdom to thy son,
And he shall wreak the traitorous wrongs of Saul:

Even as thy sin hath still importuned Heaven,
So shall thy murthers and adultery
Be punished in the sight of Israel,
As thou deserv'st, with blood, with death, and hell.
Hence, murtherer, hence!

[Throws stones and earth at **DAVID**.

ABISAI
Why doth this dead dog curse my lord the king?
Let me alone to take away his head.

DAVID
Why meddleth thus the son of Zeruia
To interrupt the action of our God?
Semei useth me with this reproach
Because the Lord hath sent him to reprove
The sins of David, printed in his brows
With blood, that blusheth for his conscience' guilt;
Who dares, then, ask him why he curseth me?

SEMEI
If, then, thy conscience tell thee thou hast sinned,
And that thy life is odious to the world,
Command thy followers to shun thy face;
And by thyself here make away thy soul,
That I may stand and glory in thy shame.

DAVID
I am not desperate, Semei, like thyself ,
But trust unto the covenant of my God,
Founded on mercy, with repentance built,
And finished with the glory of my soul.

SEMEI
A murtherer, and hope for mercy in thy end!
Hate and destruction sit upon thy brows
To watch the issue of thy damnèd ghost,
Which with thy latest gasp they'll take and tear,
Hurling in every pane of hell a piece.
Hence, murtherer, thou shame to Israel,
Foul lecher, drunkard, plague to Heaven and earth!

[Throws again at **DAVID**.

JOAB
What, is it piety in David's thoughts,
So to abhor from laws of policy

In this extremity of his distress,
To give his subjects cause of carelessness?
Send hence the dog with sorrow to his grave.

DAVID
Why should the sons of Zeruia seek to check
His spirit, which the Lord hath thus inspired?
Behold, my son which issued from my flesh,
With equal fury seeks to take my life:
How much more then the son of Jemini,
Chiefly since he doth naught but God's command?
It may be, he will look on me this day
With gracious eyes, and for his cursing bless
The heart of David in his bitterness.

SEMEI
What, dost thou fret my soul with sufferance?
O, that the souls of Isboseth and Abner,
Which thou sent'st swimming to their graves in blood,
With wounds fresh bleeding, gasping for revenge,
Were here to execute my burning hate!
But I will hunt thy foot with curses still:
Hence, monster, murtherer, mirror of contempt!

[Throws again at **DAVID**.

[Enter **AHIMAAS** and **JONATHAN**.

AHIMAAS
Long life to David, to his enemies death!

DAVID
Welcome, Ahimaäs and Jonathan:
What news sends Cusay to thy lord the king?

AHIMAAS
Cusay would wish my lord the king
To pass the river Jordan presently,
Lest he and all his people perish here;
For wise Achitophel hath counselled Absalon
To take advantage of your weary arms,
And come this night upon you in the fields.
But yet the Lord hath made his counsel scorn,
And Cusay's policy with praise preferred;
Which was to number every Israelite,
And so assault you in their pride of strength.

JONATHAN

Abiathar besides entreats the king
To send his men of war against his son,
And hazard not his person in the field.

DAVID

Thanks to Abiathar, and to you both,
And to my Cusay, whom the Lord requite;
But ten times treble thanks to his soft hand
Whose pleasant touch hath made my heart to dance,
And play him praises in my zealous breast,
That turned the counsel of Achitophel
After the prayers of his servant's lips.
Now will we pass the river all this night,
And in the morning sound the voice of war,
The voice of bloody and unkindly war.

JOAB

Then tell us how thou wilt divide thy men,
And who shall have the special charge herein.

DAVID

Joab, thyself shall for thy charge conduct
The first third part of all my valiant men;
The second shall Abisai's valour lead;
The third fair Ithay, which I most should grace
For comfort he hath done to David's woes;
And I myself will follow in the midst.

ITHAY

That let not David; for, though we should fly,
Ten thousand of us were not half so much
Esteemed with David's enemies as himself:
Thy people, loving thee, deny thee this.

DAVID

What seems them best, then, that will David do.
But now, my lords and captains, hear his voice
That never yet pierced piteous Heaven in vain;
Then let it not slip lightly through your ears; –
For my sake spare the young man Absalon.
Joab, thyself didst once use friendly words
To reconcile my heart incensed to him;
If, then, thy love be to thy kinsman sound,
And thou wilt prove a perfit Israelite,
Friend him with deeds, and touch no hair of him, –
Not that fair hair with which the wanton winds
Delight to play, and love to make it curl,
Wherein the nightingales would build their nests,

And make sweet bowers in every golden tress
To sing their lover every night asleep:
O, spoil not, Joab, Jove's fair ornaments,
Which he hath sent to solace David's soul!
The best, ye see, my lords, are swift to sin;
To sin our feet are washed with milk of roes,
And dried again with coals of lightening.
O Lord, thou see'st the proudest sin's poor slave,
And with his bridle pull'st him to the grave!
For my sake, then, spare lovely Absalon.

ITHAY
We will, my lord, for thy sake favour him.

[Exeunt.

SCENE XIII

The House of Achitophel.

Enter **ACHITOPHEL** with a halter.

ACHITOPHEL
Now hath Achitophel ordered his house,
And taken leave of every pleasure there:
Hereon depends Achitophel's delights,
And in this circle must his life be closed.
The wise Achitophel, whose counsel proved
Ever as sound for fortunate success
As if men asked the oracle of God,
Is now used like the fool of Israel:
Then set thy angry soul upon her wings,
And let her fly into the shade of death;
And for my death let Heaven for ever weep,
Making huge floods upon the land I leave,
To ravish them and all their fairest fruits.
Let all the sighs I breathed for this disgrace,
Hang on my hedges like eternal mists,
As mourning garments for their master's death.
Ope, earth, and take thy miserable son
Into the bowels of thy cursèd womb:
Once in a surfeit thou didst spew him forth;
Now for fell hunger suck him in again,
And be his body poison to thy veins.
And now, thou hellish instrument of Heaven,
Once execute th' arrest of Jove's just doom,

And stop his breast that curseth Israel.

[Exit.

SCENE XIV

The Wood of Ephraim.

Enter **ABSALON**, with **AMASA** and the rest of his train.

ABSALON
Now for the crown and throne of Israel,
To be confirmed with virtue of my sword,
And writ with David's blood upon the blade.
Now, Jove, let forth the golden firmament,
And look on him, with all thy fiery eyes,
Which thou hast made to give their glories light:
To show thou lov'st the virtue of thy hand,
Let fall a wreath of stars upon my head,
Whose influence may govern Israel
With state exceeding all her other kings.
Fight, lords and captains, that your sovereign's face
May shine in honour brighter than the sun;
And with the virtue of my beauteous rays
Make this fair land as fruitful as the fields
That with sweet milk and honey overflowed.
God, in the whissing of a pleasant wind,
Shall march upon the tops of mulberry-trees,
To cool all breasts that burn with any griefs,
As whilom he was good to Moyses' men.
By day the Lord shall sit within a cloud,
To guide your footsteps to the fields of joy;
And in the night a pillar, bright as fire,
Shall go before you, like a second sun,
Wherein the essence of his godhead is;
That day and night you may be brought to peace,
And never swarve from that delightsome path
That leads your souls to perfect happiness.
This shall he do for joy when I am king.
Then fight, brave captains, that these joys may fly
Into your bosoms with sweet victory.

[Exeunt.

SCENE XV

The Wood of Ephraim.

The battle; and then **ABSALON** hangs by the hair.

ABSALON
What angry angel, sitting in these shades,
Hath laid his cruèl hands upon my hair,
And holds my body thus 'twixt Heaven and earth?
Hath Absalon no soldier near his hand
That may untwine me this unpleasant curl,
Or wound this tree that ravisheth his lord?
O God, behold the glory of thy hand,
And choicest fruit of nature's workmanship,
Hang, like a rotten branch, upon this tree,
Fit for the axe and ready for the fire!
Since thou withhold'st all ordinary help
To loose my body from this bond of death,
O, let my beauty fill these senseless plants
With sense and power to loose me from this plague,
And work some wonder to prevent his death
Whose life thou mad'st a special miracle!

[Enter **JOAB** with a **SOLDIER**.

SOLDIER
My lord, I saw the young Prince Absalon
Hang by the hair upon a shady oak,
And could by no means get himself unloosed.

JOAB
Why slew'st thou not the wicked Absalon,
That rebel to his father and to Heaven,
That so I might have given thee for thy pains
Ten silver sickles and a golden waist?

SOLDIER
Not for a thousand shekels would I slay
The son of David, whom his father charged
Nor thou, Abisai, nor the son of Gath,
Should touch with stroke of deadly violence.
The charge was given in hearing of us all;
And, had I done it, then, I know, thyself,
Before thou wouldst abide the king's rebuke,
Wouldst have accused me as a man of death.

JOAB

I must not now stand trifling here with thee.

ABSALON
Help, Joab, help, O, help thy Absalon!
Let not thy angry thoughts be laid in blood,
In blood of him that sometimes nourished thee,
And softened thy sweet heart with friendly love:
O, give me once again my father's sight,
My dearest father and my princely sovereign!
That, shedding tears of blood before his face,
The ground may witness, and the heavens record,
My last submission sound and full of ruth.

JOAB
Rebel to nature, hate to Heaven and earth!
Shall I give help to him that thirsts the soul
Of his dear father and my sovereign lord?
Now see, the Lord hath tangled in a tree
The health and glory of thy stubborn heart,
And made thy pride curbed with a senseless plant:
Now, Absalon, how doth the Lord regard
The beauty whereupon thy hope was built,
And which thou thought'st his grace did glory in?
Find'st thou not now, with fear of instant death,
That God affects not any painted shape
Or goodly personage, when the virtuous soul
Is stuffed with naught but pride and stubbornness?
But, preach I to thee, while I should revenge
Thy cursèd sin that staineth Israel,
And makes her fields blush with her children's blood?
Take that as part of thy deservèd plague,
Which worthily no torment can inflict.

[Stabs him.

ABSALON
O Joab, Joab, cruèl, ruthless Joab!
Herewith thou wound'st thy kingly sovereign's heart,
Whose heavenly temper hates his children's blood,
And will be sick, I know, for Absalon. –
O, my dear father, that thy melting eyes
Might pierce this thicket to behold thy son,
Thy dearest son, gored with a mortal dart!
Yet, Joab, pity me: pity my father, Joab;
Pity his soul's distress that mourns my life,
And will be dead, I know, to hear my death.

JOAB

If he were so remorseful of thy state,
Why sent he me against thee with the sword?
All Joab means to pleasure thee withal
Is to despatch thee quickly of thy pain:
Hold, Absalon, Joab's pity is in this;
In this, proud Absalon, is Joab's love.

[Stabs him again; and then exit with **SOLDIER**.

ABSALON
Such love, such pity Israel's God send thee,
And for his love to David pity me!
Ah, my dear father, see thy bowels bleed;
See death assault thy dearest Absalon;
See, pity, pardon, pray for Absalon!

[Enter **FIVE** or **SIX SOLDIERS**.

1st SOLDIER
See where the rebel in his glory hangs. –
Where is the virtue of thy beauty, Absalon?
Will any of us here now fear thy looks,
Or be in love with that thy golden hair
Wherein was wrapt rebellion 'gainst thy sire,
And cords prepared to stop thy father's breath?
Our captain Joab hath begun to us;
And here's an end to thee and all thy sins.

[They stab **ABSALON**; who dies.

Come, let us take the beauteous rebel down,
And in some ditch, amids this darksome wood,
Bury his bulk beneath a heap of stones,
Whose stony heart did hunt his father's death.

[Re-enter, in triumph with drum and ensign, **JOAB**; **ABISAI** and **SOLDIERS**.

JOAB
Well done, tall soldiers! take the traitor down,
And in this miry ditch inter his bones,
Covering his hateful breast with heaps of stones.
This shady thicket of dark Ephrami
Shall ever lower on his cursèd grave;
Night-ravens and owls shall ring his fatal knell,
And sit exclaiming on his damnèd soul;
There shall they heap their preys of carrion,
Till all his grave be clad with stinking bones,
That it may loathe the sense of every man:

So shall his end breed horror to his name,
And to his traitorous fact eternal shame.

[Exeunt.

Enter **CHORUS**.

CHORUS
O dreadful president of his just doom,
Whose holy heart is never touched with ruth
Of fickle beauty or of glorious shapes,
But with the virtue of an upright soul,
Humble and zealous in his inward thoughts,
Though in his person loathsome and deformed!
Now, since this story lends us other store,
To make a third discourse of David's life,
Adding thereto his most renownèd death,
And all their deaths that at his death he judged,
Here end we this, and what here wants to please,
We will supply with treble willingness.

[Exit.

SCENE XVI

Near the Battlefield.

Trumpets sound.

Enter **JOAB, AHIMAAS, CUSAY; AMASA**, with all the other **FOLLOWERS** of Absalon.

JOAB
Soldiers of Israel, and ye sons of Judah,
That have contended in these irksome broils,
And ript old Israel's bowels with your swords;
The godless general of your stubborn arms
Is brought by Israel's helper to the grave,
A grave of shame, and scorn of all the tribes:
Now, then, to save your honours from the dust,
And keep your bloods in temper by your bones,
Let Joab's ensign shroud your manly heads,
Direct your eyes, your weapons, and your hearts,

To guard the life of David from his foes.
Error hath masked your much-too-forward minds,
And you have sinned against the chosen state,
Against his life, for whom your lives are blessed,
And followed an usurper to the field;
In whose just death your deaths are threatenèd;
But Joab pities your disordered souls,
And therefore offers pardon, peace, and love,
To all that will be friendly reconciled
To Israel's weal, to David, and to Heaven. –
Amasa, thou art leader of the host
That under Absalon have raised their arms;
Then be a captain wise and politic,
Careful and loving for thy soldiers' lives,
And lead them to this honourable league.

AMASA
I will; at least, I'll do my best:
And for the gracious offer thou hast made
I give thee thanks, as much as for my head. –
Then, you deceived poor souls of Israel,
Since now ye see the errors you incurred,
With thanks and due submission be appeased;
And as ye see your captain's president,
Here cast we, then, our swords at Joab's feet,
Submitting with all zeal and reverence
Our goods and bodies to his gracious hands.

[Kneels with others.

JOAB
Stand up, and take ye all your swords again:

[All stand up.

David and Joab shall be blessed herein.

AHIMAAS
Now let me go inform my lord the king
How God hath freed him from his enemies.

JOAB
Another time, Ahimaäs, not now. –
But, Cusay, go thyself, and tell the king
The happy message of our good success.

CUSAY
I will, my lord, and thank thee for thy grace.

[Exit.

AHIMAAS
What if thy servant should go too, my lord?

JOAB
What news hast thou to bring since he is gone?

AHIMAAS
Yet do Ahimaäs so much content,
That he may run about so sweet a charge.

JOAB
Run, if thou wilt; and peace be with thy steps. –

[Exit AHIMAAS.

Now follow, that you may salute the king
With humble hearts and reconcilèd souls.

AMASA
We follow, Joab, to our gracious king;
And him our swords shall honour to our deaths.

[Exeunt.

SCENE XVII

David's Headquarters at Manahaim.

Enter **DAVID**, **BETHSABE**, **SALOMON**, **CHILEAB**, **ADONIA**, and **NATHAN**, with their train.

BETHSABE
What means my lord, the lamp of Israel,
From whose bright eyes all eyes receive their light,
To dim the glory of his sweet aspécts,
And paint his countenance with his heart's distress?
Why should his thoughts retain a sad conceit,
When every pleasure kneels before his throne,
And sues for sweet acceptance with his grace?
Take but your lute, and make the mountains dance,
Retrieve the sun's sphere, and restrain the clouds,
Give ears to trees, make savage lions tame,
Impose still silence to the loudest winds,
And fill the fairest day with foulest storms:

Then why should passions of much meaner power
Bear head against the heart of Israel?

DAVID
Fair Bethsabe, thou mightst increase the strength
Of these thy arguments, drawn from my skill,
By urging thy sweet sight to my conceits,
Whose virtue ever served for sacred balm
To cheer my pinings past all earthly joys:
But, Bethsabe, the daughter of the Highest,
Whose beauty builds the towers of Israel,
She that in chains of pearl and unicorn
Leads at her train the ancient golden world.
The world that Adam held in paradise,
Whose breath refineth all infectious airs,
And makes the meadows smile at her repair, –
She, she, my dearest Bethsabe,
Fair Peace, the goddess of our graces here,
Is fled the streets of fair Jerusalem,
The fields of Israel, and the heart of David,
Leading my comforts in her golden chains,
Linked to the life and soul of Absalon.

BETHSABE
Then is the pleasure of my sovereign's heart
So wrapt within the bosom of that son,
That Salomon, whom Israel's God affects,
And gave the name unto him for his love,
Should be no salve to comfort David's soul?

DAVID
Salomon, my love, is David's lord;
Our God hath named him lord of Israel:
In him (for that, and since he is thy son,)
Must David needs be pleasèd at the heart;
And he shall surely sit upon my throne.
But Absalon, the beauty of my bones,
Fair Absalon, the counterfeit of love,
Sweet Absalon, the image of content,
Must claim a portion in his father's care,
And be in life and death King David's son.

NATHAN
Yet, as my lord hath said, let Salomon reign,
Whom God in naming hath anointed king.
Now is he apt to learn th' eternal laws,
Whose knowledge being rooted in his youth
Will beautify his age with glorious fruits;

While Absalon, incensed with graceless pride,
Usurps and stains the kingdom with his sin:
Let Salomon be made thy staff of age,
Fair Israel's rest, and honour of thy race.

DAVID
Tell me, my Salomon, wilt thou embrace
Thy father's precepts gravèd in thy heart,
And satisfy my zeal to thy renown
With practice of such sacred principles
As shall concern the state of Israel?

SALOMON
My royal father, if the heavenly zeal,
Which for my welfare feeds upon your soul,
Were not sustained with virtue of mine own;
If the sweet accents of your cheerful voice
Should not each hour beat upon mine ears
As sweetly as the breath of Heaven to him
That gaspeth scorchèd with the summer's sun;
I should be guilty of unpardoned sin,
Fearing the plague of Heaven and shame of earth:
But since I vow myself to learn the skill
And holy secrets of his mighty hand
Whose cunning tunes the music of my soul,
It would content me, father, first to learn
How the Eternal framed the firmament;
Which bodies lead their influence by fire,
And which are filled with hoary winter's ice;
What sign is rainy, and what star is fair;
Why by the rules of true proportiön
The year is still divided into months,
The months to days, the days to certain hours;
What fruitful race shall fill the future world;
Or for what time shall this round building stand;
What magistrates, what kings shall keep in awe
Men's minds with bridles of th' eternal law.

DAVID
Wade not too far, my boy, in waves too deep:
The feeble eyes of our aspiring thoughts
Behold things present, and record things past;
But things to come exceed our human reach,
And are not painted yet in angels' eyes:
For those, submit thy sense, and say – "Thou power,
That now art framing of the future world,
Know'st all to come, not by the course of Heaven,
By frail conjectures of inferior signs,

By monstrous floods, by flights and flocks of birds,
By bowels of a sacrificèd beast,
Or by the figures of some hidden art;
But by a true and natural presage,
Laying the ground and perfect architect
Of all our actions now before thine eyes,
From Adam to the end of Adam's seed:
O Heaven, protect my weakness with thy strength!
So look on me that I may view thy face,
And see these secrets written in thy brows.
O sun, come dart thy rays upon my moon!
That now mine eyes, eclipsèd to the earth,
May brightly be refined and shine to Heaven;
Transform me from this flesh, that I may live,
Before my death, regenerate with thee.
O thou great God, ravish my earthly sprite!
That for the time a more than human skill
May feed the organons of all my sense;
That, when I think, thy thoughts may be my guide,
And, when I speak, I may be made by choice
The perfect echo of thy heavenly voice."
Thus say, my son, and thou shalt learn them all.

SALOMON
A secret fury ravisheth my soul,
Lifting my mind above her human bounds;
And, as the eagle, rousèd from her stand
With violent hunger, towering in the air,
Seizeth her feathered prey, and thinks to feed,
But seeing then a cloud beneath her feet,
Lets fall the fowl, and is emboldened
With eyes intentive to bedare the sun,
And styeth close unto his stately sphere;
So Salomon, mounted on the burning wings
Of zeal divine, lets fall his mortal food,
And cheers his senses with celestial air,
Treads in the golden starry labyrinth,
And holds his eyes fixed on Jehovah's brows.
Good father, teach me further what to do.

NATHAN
See, David, how his haughty spirit mounts,
Even now of height to wield a diadem:
Then make him promise that he may succeed,
And rest old Israel's bones from broils of war.

DAVID
Nathan, thou prophet, sprung from Jesse's root,

I promise thee and lovely Bethsabe,
My Salomon shall govern after me.

BETHSABE
He that hath touched thee with this righteous thought
Preserve the harbour of thy thoughts in peace!

[Enter **MESSENGER**.

MESSENGER
My lord, thy servants of the watch have seen
One running hitherward from forth the wars,

DAVID
If he be come alone, he bringeth news.

MESSENGER
Another hath thy servant seen, my lord,
Whose running much resembles Sadoc's son.

DAVID
He is a good man, and good tidings brings.

[Enter **AHIMAAS**.

AHIMAAS
Peace and content be with my lord the king,
Whom Israel's God hath blessed with victory.

DAVID
Tell me, Ahimaas, lives my Absalon?

AHIMAAS
I saw a troop of soldiers gatherèd,
But know not what the tumult might import.

DAVID
Stand by, until some other may inform
The heart of David with a happy truth.

[Enter **CUSAY**.

CUSAY
Happiness and honour live with David's soul,
Whom God hath blessed with conquest of his foes

DAVID
But, Cusay, lives the young man Absalon?

CUSAY

The stubborn enemies to David's peace,
And all that cast their darts against his crown,
Fare ever like the young man Absalon!
For as he rid the woods of Ephraïm,
Which fought for thee as much as all thy men,
His hair was tangled in a shady oak;
And hanging there, by Joab and his men
Sustained the stroke of well-deservèd death.

DAVID

Hath Absalon sustained the stroke of death?
Die, David, for the death of Absalon,
And make these cursèd news the bloody darts
That through his bowels rip thy wretched breast.
Hence, David, walk the solitary woods,
And in some cedar's shade the thunder slew,
And fire from Heaven hath made his branches black,
Sit mourning the decease of Absalon:
Against the body of that blasted plant
In thousand shivers break thy ivory lute,
Hanging thy stringless harp upon his boughs;
And through the hollow sapless sounding trunk
Bellow the torments that perplex thy soul.
There let the winds sit sighing till they burst;
Let tempest, muffled with a cloud of pitch,
Threaten the forests with her hellish face,
And, mounted fiercely on her iron wings,
Rend up the wretched engine by the roots
That held my dearest Absalon to death.
Then let them toss my broken lute to Heaven,
Even to his hands that beats me with the strings,
To show how sadly his poor shepherd sings.

[Goes to his pavilion and sits close a while.

BETHSABE

Die, Bethsabe, to see thy David mourn,
To hear his tunes of anguish and of hell.
O, help, my David, help thy Bethsabe,

[She kneels down.

Whose heart is piercèd with thy breathy swords,
And bursts with burden of ten thousand griefs!
Now sit thy sorrows sucking of my blood:
O, that it might be poison to their powers,

And that their lips might draw my bosom dry,
So David's love might ease him, though she die!

NATHAN
These violent passions come not from above;
David and Bethsabe offend the Highest,
To mourn in this immeasurable sort.

DAVID [Looking forth.]
O Absalon, Absalon! O my son, my son!
Would God that I had died for Absalon!
But he is dead; ah, dead! Absalon is dead:
And David lives to die for Absalon.

[Sits close again.

[Enter **JOAB**, **ABISAI**, **ITHAY**, and their train.

JOAB
Why lies the queen so prostrate on the ground?
Why is this company so tragic-hued?
Why is the king now absent from his men,
And marcheth not in triumph through the gates?

[Unfolds the pavilion.

David, awake; if sleep have shut thine eyes,
Sleep of affection, that thou canst not see
The honour offered to the victor's head:
Joab brings conquest piercèd on his spear,
And joy from all the tribes of Israel.

DAVID
Thou man of blood, thou sepulchre of death,
Whose marble breast intomb[s] my bowels quick,
Did I not charge thee, nay, entreat thy hand,
Even for my sake, to spare my Absalon?
And hast thou now, in spite of David's health,
And scorn to do my heart some happiness,
Given him the sword and spilt his purple soul?

JOAB
What, irks it David, that he victor breathes,
That Judah and the fields of Israel
Should cleanse their faces from their children's blood?
What, art thou weary of thy royal rule?
Is Israel's throne a serpent in thine eyes,
And he that set thee there so far from thanks,

That thou must curse his servant for his sake?
Hast thou not said that, as the morning light,
The cloudless morning, so should be thine house,
And not as flowers by the brightest rain
Which grow up quickly and as quickly fade?
Hast thou not said, the wicked are as thorns,
That cannot be preservèd with the hand,
And that the man shall touch them must be armed
With coats of iron and garments made of steel,
Or with the shaft of a defencèd spear?
And art thou angry he is now cut off
That led the guiltless swarming to their deaths,
And was more wicked than an host of men?
Advance thee from thy melancholy den,
And deck thy body with thy blissful robes,
Or, by the Lord that sways the Heaven I swear,
I'll lead thine armies to another king
Shall cheer them for their princely chivalry,
And not sit daunted, frowning in the dark,
When his fair looks, with oil and wine refreshed,
Should dart into their bosoms gladsome beams,
And fill their stomachs with triumphant feasts;
That when elsewhere stern war shall sound his trump,
And call another battle to the field,
Fame still may bring thy valiant soldiers home,
And for their service happily confess
She wanted worthy trumps to sound their prowess:
Take thou this course and live; refuse and die.

ABISAI
Come, brother, let him sit there till he sink;
Some other shall advance the name of Joab.

[Offers to go out with **JOAB**.

BETHSABE [Rising]
O, stay, my lords, stay! David mourns no more,
But riseth to give honour to your acts.

DAVID [Rising, and coming from his pavilion]
Then happy art thou, David's fairest son,
That, freèd from the yoke of earthly toils,
And séquestered from sense of human sins,
Thy soul shall joy the sacred cabinet
Of those divine ideas that present
Thy changèd spirit with a Heaven of bliss.
Then thou art gone; ah, thou art gone, my son!
To Heaven, I hope, my Absalon is gone:

Thy soul there placed in honour of the saints,
Or angels clad with immortality,
Shall reap a sevenfold grace for all thy griefs;
Thy eyes, now no more eyes but shining stars,
Shall deck the flaming heavens with novel lamps;
There shalt thou taste the drink of seraphins,
And cheer thy feelings with archangels' food;
Thy day of rest, thy holy sabbath-day,
Shall be eternal; and, the curtain drawn,
Thou shalt behold thy sovereign face to face,
With wonder, knit in triple unity,
Unity infinite and innumerable –
Courage, brave captains! Joab's tale hath stirred,
And made the suit of Israel preferred.

JOAB
Bravely resolved, and spoken like a king:
Now may old Israel and his daughters sing.

[Exeunt **OMNES**.